WHERE'S THE DUDE?

THE GREAT MOVIE SPOTTING CHALLENGE

SHARM MURUGIAH & ADAM WOODWARD

LAURENCE KING PUBLISHING

TITANIC

KILL BILL: VOLUME I

APOCALYPSE NOW

ROCKY

JAWS

WILLY WONKA &
THE CHOCOLATE FACTORY

BEN-HUR

FERRIS BUELLER'S DAY OFF

PLANET OF THE APES

FOUR WEDDINGS AND A FUNERAL

THE GRAND BUDAPEST HOTEL

THE WIZARD OF OZ

You know The Dude. As the hapless hero of the Coen brothers' 1998 comedy, *The Big Lebowski*, he's become something of an unlikely pop culture icon - the kind of fella everyone can admire, if not necessarily aspire to.

Yet while he's most definitely a pacifist at heart, The Dude is not a man to sit idly by when a couple of thugs ransack his home and steal his most prized possession - his rug. Only trouble is, he seems to have gotten a little lost himself.

Where's The Dude? sees cinema's most lovable burn-out shamble his way through movie history, trying his best not to draw too much attention to himself, all in search of his missing rug.

See if you can spot The Dude in all 12 scenes, then go back and look for the famous faces, props and characters connected to each film.

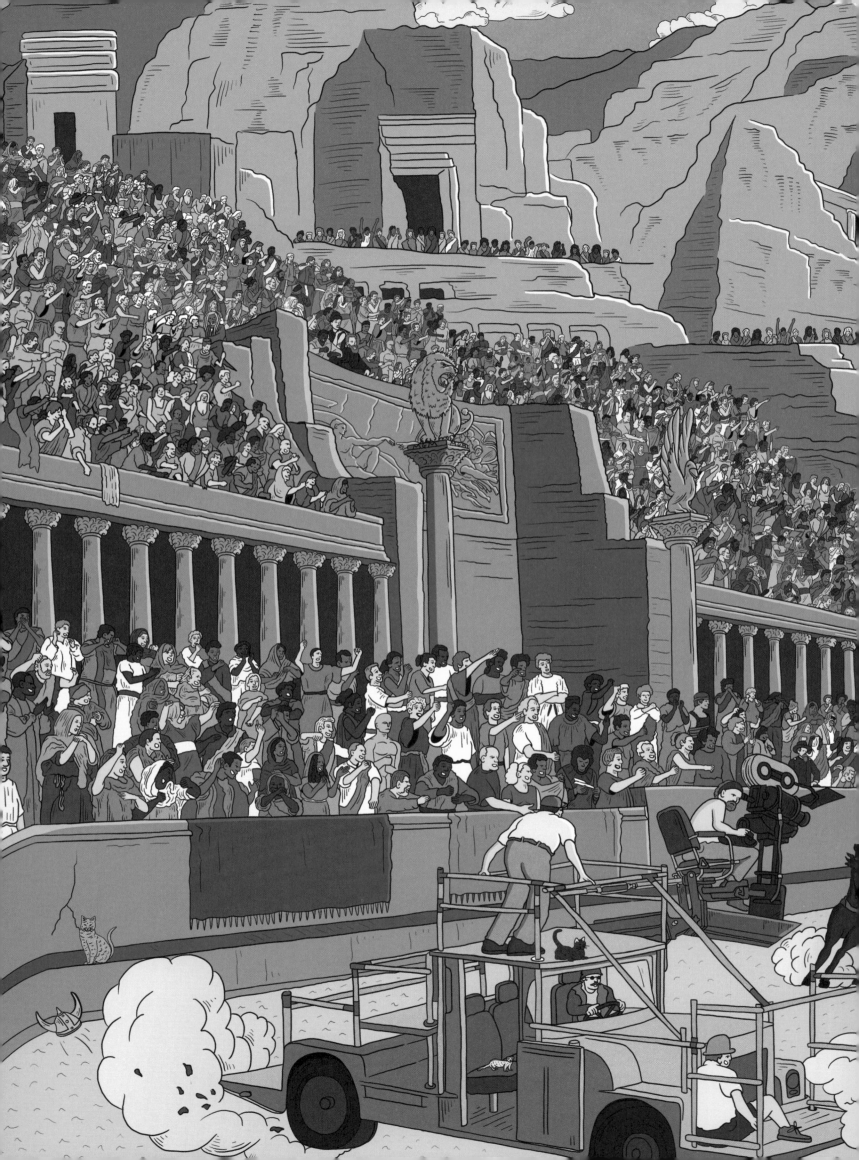

TITANIC (1997)

After fulfilling a personal ambition by visiting the wreck of the RMS *Titanic*, director **James Cameron** [1] pitched his 'Romeo & Juliet on the *Titanic*' to 20th Century Fox. In order to bring his vision to life, however, he needed to find the perfect young leads. **Matthew McConaughey** [2] was initially considered for the part of Jack Dawson before **Leonardo DiCaprio** [3] landed the life-changing role, while **Kate Winslet** [3] saw off Gwyneth Paltrow and Claire Danes to kick-start her career as Rose DeWitt Bukater.

This wasn't the first time the story of the *Titanic* had been told on the big screen, though it's fair to say that 1958's *A Night to Remember*, starring British actor **Kenneth More** [4], didn't lodge itself in the collective consciousness in quite the same way. Nor, for that matter, did **Kevin Costner**'s [5] *The Postman*, which was released the same week as Cameron's Oscar-sweeping hit and subsequently failed to deliver at the box office. But it wasn't all plain sailing for Cameron that awards season - he shared the 1996 Razzie for Worst Screenplay with **Sylvester Stallone** [6] for *Rambo: First Blood Part II*.

In addition to becoming the highest-grossing film ever made, *Titanic* broke further records, with **Céline Dion**'s [7] inescapable theme song 'My Heart Will Go On' shifting upwards of 15 million copies globally. Things could have been so different had Cameron's first choice of musical collaborator said yes, although there remains a distinct **Enya** [8] flavour to the original score by **James Horner** [9], whom Cameron had previously worked with on 1986's *Aliens*. Listen carefully and you'll notice further homages, most notably in the immortal line 'I'd rather be his whore than your wife', first spoken by **Norma Jennings** [10] in *Twin Peaks* and repeated here by Winslet to **Billy Zane** [11]. Who knew James Cameron was secretly a David Lynch fan?

The film features period-specific cultural references too, such as Rose's mention of **Sigmund Freud** [12] during another delicious put-down. There's also **Kathy Bates**'s [13] sharp-tongued socialite Molly Brown, based on an actual passenger who escaped aboard a lifeboat and became known posthumously as 'The Unsinkable Molly Brown'. In another nod to a real-life survivor, the **Pomeranian** [14] owned by Gloria Stuart's Old Rose is the same breed of dog as one rescued from the sinking ship. Despite this meticulous attention to detail, Cameron did manage to upset famed astrophysicist **Neil deGrasse Tyson** [15], who emailed the director pointing out the inaccurate configuration of the stars during the climactic scene where Rose clings to a piece of driftwood. Fifteen years later, Cameron responded by re-editing the film in time for its 3D re-release.

Can you also spot... The T-800 [16], a Xenomorph [17], a Na'vi [18], 'Madame Bijoux' from Jack's sketchbook [19], and another French girl drawn by an artist, Édouard Manet's *A Bar at the Folies-Bergère* [20].

Has The Dude given you the slip? Here's a clue: top middle, to the right of Walter Sobchak

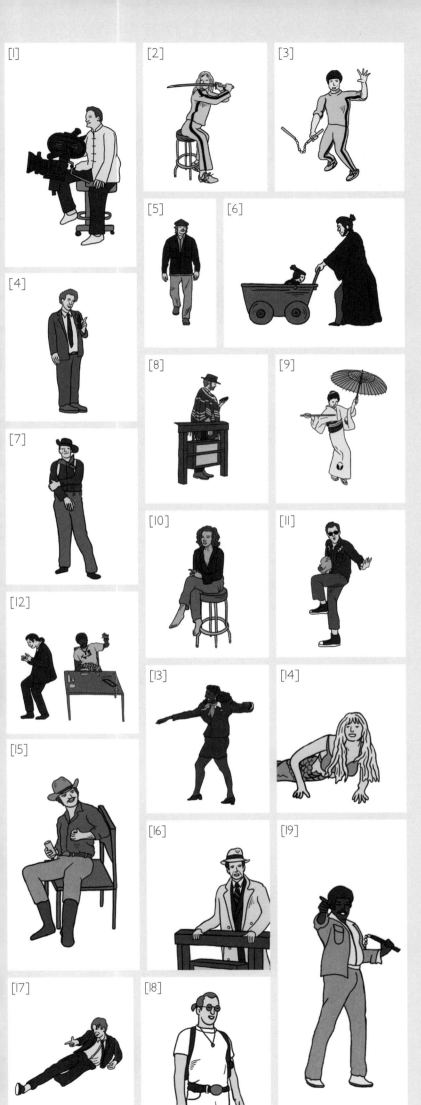

KILL BILL: VOLUME I (2003)

Quentin Tarantino [1] is a filmmaker who wears his influences on his claret-splattered sleeve, and his two-part martial arts extravaganza is no exception. By far the clearest pastiche in *Kill Bill* is **Uma Thurman**'s [2] iconic yellow jumpsuit, which Tarantino borrowed from 1978's *Game of Death* – the film **Bruce Lee** [3] never got to finish. Chinese director Stephen Chow Sing-chi did something similar in his 2001 martial arts/sports comedy hybrid *Shaolin Soccer*. Being the pop culture magpie that he is, *Kill Bill* contains far subtler nods to many of Tarantino's favourite films, from Michael Madsen echoing **Bruce Dern**'s [4] line, 'I'm gonna catch me the cowboy that's never been caught', from 1978's *The Driver*, to the poster for the 1974 **Charles Bronson** [5] vehicle *Mr. Majestyk* appearing in Budd's trailer, to the moment when Tomisaburô Wakayama's **Lone Wolf** [6] from *Shogun Assassin* is glimpsed on a television screen in Bill's villa.

Look closely and you may also spot an homage to **John Wayne** [7] in the 1956 western *The Searchers*, another to **Clint Eastwood** [8] in *The Good, The Bad and the Ugly* from 1966, and a tribute to **Meiko Kaji** [9] in 1973's *Lady Snowblood* in the form of Lucy Liu's deadly assassin O-Ren Ishii. The references don't end there, as the closing shot of Thurman's *The Bride* will be familiar to fans of the 1933 historical drama *Queen Christina*, starring **Greta Garbo** [10] as the titular Swedish monarch. Bizarrely enough, **Johnny Knoxville** [11] is even said to have inspired Tarantino, with *Jackass: The Movie* supposedly having some bearing on *Kill Bill*'s chaotic style.

Tarantino is a self-confessed film buff, and it's his extensive cinematic knowledge that makes him so adept at casting actors against type or else plucking them from seeming obscurity, often reviving their careers in the process. It certainly did the trick for **John Travolta** [12], who teamed up with **Samuel L. Jackson** [12] to such potent effect in *Pulp Fiction*, and **Pam Grier** [13] in *Jackie Brown*, whose earlier film *Coffy* was watched by the cast and crew of *Kill Bill* before filming. In Tarantino's fourth feature it was the turn of **Daryl Hannah** [14], the American actress previously best known for her work in *Blade Runner* and *Splash*. Given his reputation for getting the best out of actors deemed to be past their prime, it's surprising that anyone would turn Tarantino down, but that's exactly what **Burt Reynolds** [15] did when offered the part of Bill. **Warren Beatty** [16] also spurned the writer/director, though at least he redeemed himself by recommending David Carradine for the part.

Can you also spot... Tim Roth in *Reservoir Dogs* [17], Woody Harrelson in *Natural Born Killers* [18], and Michael Jai White, who filmed a fight sequence for *Kill Bill* that ended up on the cutting room floor [19].

Has The Dude given you the slip?
Here's a clue: middle left, behind the staircase

APOCALYPSE NOW (1979)

Given the well-chronicled madness of the Vietnam War, it seems fitting that Francis Ford Coppola's film was a somewhat traumatic experience for those involved. That's certainly the main takeaway from **Eleanor Coppola**'s [1] making-of documentary *Hearts of Darkness: A Filmmaker's Apocalypse*, so-called after **Joseph Conrad**'s [2] 1899 novella on which her husband's film was loosely based. Another literary inspiration was **T.S. Eliot** [3], whose poem *The Hollow Men* is read aloud by **Marlon Brando**'s [4] Kurtz towards the end of the film. Brando's contribution to *Apocalypse Now* is especially telling, as his brief but extraordinary performance was reportedly entirely at odds with his attitude on set, with Coppola accusing him of turning up overweight, underprepared and angling for a salary increase. Sadly we'll never know how things might have turned out had Coppola's first choice for the role, **Orson Welles** [5], signed up, but at least we'll always have **John Malkovich** [6] in Nicolas Roeg's 1983 *Heart of Darkness* for a different take on the character.

In other 'what if?' casting scenarios, **Steve McQueen** [7] was the first to turn down the role of Captain Willard, with **Al Pacino** [8] following suit as a result of him falling ill while filming scenes for *The Godfather: Part II* in the Dominican jungle. **Clint Eastwood** [9] was also considered, but distanced himself from the project after expressing concerns over the darkness of the script. **Harvey Keitel** [10] almost ended up in the film too, but was fired because Coppola didn't like the way he was playing the part. His replacement **Martin Sheen** [11] suffered a heart attack midway through production, resulting in his brother **Joe Estevez** [12] standing in to perform Willard's voice-over. *Apocalypse Now* also introduced cinema audiences to **Laurence Fishburne** [13], who secured the part of Tyrone 'Clean' Miller after lying about his age.

For all that *Apocalypse Now* is a film with a big fat asterisk next to it thanks to its turbulent production, it remains a hugely influential work that was widely lauded upon release. Indeed, Coppola earned the recognition of his peers when the film premiered at the 1979 Cannes Film Festival, sharing the coveted Palme d'Or with *The Tin Drum* director **Volker Schlöndorff** [14]. So many aspects of Coppola's film have become ingrained in popular culture, not least the inspired soundtrack, which evokes images of war through **Richard Wagner**'s [15] stirring 'Ride of the Valkyries' and **Jim Morrison**'s [16] haunting vocal on The Doors' 'The End'.

Can you also spot... Charlie Sheen in *Platoon* [17], producer Roger Corman, who gave Coppola his start in the industry [18], *Playboy* founder Hugh Hefner [19], and Louis Fieser, the US chemist who invented napalm [20].

Has The Dude given you the slip? Here's a clue: top right, lounging in a hammock

ROCKY (1976)

The story goes that before he sold his *Rocky* script to United Artists in 1975, **Sylvester Stallone** [1] was so broke that he was forced to sell his beloved **pet pooch** [2] outside a liquor store for $40. Once the film's production was underway, he bought back his bullmastiff, Butkus, for $15,000 so it could star alongside him. Like so many rags-to-riches legends, Stallone's has been embellished over time, but the basic facts of his unlikely rise are true - in reality he gave Butkus away to a family only to borrow him back for use in the film and its 1979 sequel.

Rocky earned Stallone two Academy Award nominations, transforming not just the fortunes of its 30-year-old star but also those of his younger brother **Frank** [3], who was handed a small cameo. The film bagged three Oscars in total including Best Picture, beating *All the President's Men, Network, Bound for Glory* and *Taxi Driver*, for which **Robert De Niro** [4] also received a Best Actor nomination. It is one of two boxing movies to claim Hollywood's top prize, the other being **Clint Eastwood**'s [5] *Million Dollar Baby* from 2004.

Things could have been so different had the studio got its way and cast Burt Reynolds in the lead, but Stallone's determination ensured that it would be his image immortalized in bronze outside the Philadelphia Museum of Art, overlooking a monument to another American hero, **George Washington** [6]. *Rocky* proved a turning point in the careers of many of those involved in its making, not least **Francis Ford Coppola**'s [7] sister Talia Shire, who pipped Susan Sarandon and **Cher** [8] to the part of Adrian, director John G. Avildsen, whose run of iconic film characters continued with **Mr. Miyagi** [9] in 1984's *The Karate Kid*, and **Carl Weathers** [10], who landed his big break when real-life boxer Ken Norton decided against playing Apollo Creed.

It's likely that Norton's change of heart was due to Creed being based on **Muhammad Ali** [11], whom he fought three times between 1973 and 1976. Yet Norton was not the only former pro to reject *Rocky* - of all the former heavyweight champs who were invited to appear in the film, only **Joe Frazier** [12] obliged. Just as it is impossible to envision anyone else as the eponymous pugilist, Weathers made the character his own, launching a successful career off the back of his performance and later teaming up with Arnold Schwarzenegger to take on the **Predator** [13]. *Rocky* continues to work its star-making magic, with Michael B. Jordan graduating from the 2015 spin-off, *Creed*, to Marvel's **Black Panther** [14].

Can you also spot... Mr. T in *Rocky III* [15], boxing promoter Don King [16], ring announcer Michael Buffer [17], Albert Einstein, who Paulie compares to Rocky [18], Paulie's birthday robot from *Rocky IV* [19], and James Brown in the same movie [20].

Here's a clue: upper right, next to Apollo Creed's banner

Has The Dude given you the slip?

JAWS (1975)

It's one of the most successful films ever made, but the making of *Jaws* was far from smooth sailing. Producers Richard D. Zanuck and David Brown bought the rights to **Peter Benchley**'s [1] 1974 novel before it was even released, so confident were they that it would make a good movie. After promising Benchley that he would be allowed to write the screenplay, his draft was turned over to TV writer Carl Gottlieb and a promising 26-year-old director named **Steven Spielberg** [2]. Universal Pictures originally wanted John 'Safe Hands' Sturges to helm the project, a veteran Hollywood filmmaker whose credits include an adaptation of **Ernest Hemingway**'s [3] *The Old Man and the Sea*, from which Gottlieb coincidentally took inspiration for *Jaws*.

At one stage the studio offered the job to Dick Richards, only to let him go when it transpired that he didn't know the difference between a shark and a whale. After all, they weren't making **Moby Dick** [4], though in fairness the fishing vessel captained by Quint was christened **'Orca'** [5] after the great white's only natural predator. Spielberg eventually got the call after outlining a very different vision for the film, placing greater emphasis on the chase sequences. He made some significant changes to the cast, too, rejecting **Charlton Heston** [6] for the role of Quint after **Robert Mitchum** [7] had turned him down. Spielberg eventually settled on Robert Shaw to appear alongside **Roy Scheider** [8] and Richard Dreyfuss, the latter going on to star in *Close Encounters of the Third Kind* and *Stand by Me* as one of the grown-up **kids** [9].

There's an old adage in Hollywood that says never work with children and animals, but while **Spielberg's pet dog Elmer** [10] was perfectly well-behaved on set, the mechanical shark used for the film was notoriously temperamental. So much so, in fact, that he dubbed it 'Bruce' after **his lawyer** [11], a titbit of film trivia alluded to in Pixar's *Finding Nemo* [12]. Bruce didn't just cause headaches for Spielberg either - his longtime friend and frequent collaborator **George Lucas** [13] got his head stuck in a prop shark during filming.

While *Jaws* is credited for ushering in the modern-day blockbuster, it also birthed four regrettable sequels, the worst being 1987's *Jaws: The Revenge*, which star **Michael Caine** [14] refers to as one of his 'paycheck pictures'. Still, the singular genius of Spielberg's original remains untarnished to this day. Few films have served as a source of inspiration to so many - even **Fidel Castro** [15] was a fan, the late Cuban leader having once praised *Jaws* for its 'anti-capitalism message' . . .

Can you also spot... E.T. [16], Richard Kiel as James Bond villain Jaws [17], Harrison Ford as Indiana Jones [18], Michael J. Fox in *Back to the Future* [19], and Olivia Newton-John, whose song 'I Honestly Love You' can be heard in the beach scene [20].

Has The Dude given you the slip? **Here's a clue:** upper left, behind George Lucas

[1] [2] [3]
[4] [5] [6]
[7] [8] [9] [10]
[11] [12]
[13]
[14] [15] [16] [17]
[18] [19] [20]

WILLY WONKA & THE CHOCOLATE FACTORY (1971)

Adored by fans but despised by its author, *Willy Wonka & the Chocolate Factory* is a film of strange contradictions. **Roald Dahl** [1] was so unhappy with director Mel Stuart's take on his 1964 children's novel, in fact, that he refused to sell him the rights to the book's sequel, *Charlie and the Great Glass Elevator*. Early disputes centred around the cast - all six performing members of **Monty Python** [2] put themselves forward for the role of Willy Wonka, but Dahl wanted **Spike Milligan** [3], whose *Goon Show* co-star **Peter Sellers** [4] is said to have begged the British writer to be in the film. It's not the only time the title character would prove contentious, thanks to **Johnny Depp**'s [5] divisive performance in Tim Burton's 2005 adaptation.

It's hard to imagine anyone but **Gene Wilder** [6] playing the part, if nothing else simply because he invested so much of his own inimitable persona into the character. Wilder had already made his name four years earlier in **Mel Brooks**'s [7] *The Producers*, and later brought the house down in *Young Frankenstein*, *Blazing Saddles*, also by Brooks, and *Silver Streak*, the first of his fruitful collaborations with fellow funny man **Richard Pryor** [8]. But he will always be remembered as the sweet-toothed entrepreneur who encouraged viewers young and old to let their imaginations run wild.

Many of Dahl's best-loved works have been turned into films, most notably 1990's *The Witches*, starring **Anjelica Huston** [9], 1996's *Matilda* with **Danny DeVito** [10], and the live-action animated adventure *James and the Giant Peach* from the same year [11]. Oddly enough, the adaptation rights for *Charlie and the Chocolate Factory* were held by the American cereal conglomerate **Quaker Oats** [12], who were keen to promote a new chocolate bar they were developing. They helped to finance the film and used the opportunity to launch a number of tie-in snacks.

Dahl also created the sinister **Child Catcher** [13] from the 1968 musical caper *Chitty Chitty Bang Bang*. And speaking of all things unsettling, keep your eyes peeled during the infamous tunnel sequence in *Willy Wonka & the Chocolate Factory* and you may catch a glimpse of **Walon Green** [14], the American documentary filmmaker and writer who penned the screenplay for Sam Peckinpah's seminal western *The Wild Bunch*.

Amid all the weird and wonderful footnotes there are several curious musical connections too. The melodic code used by Willy Wonka to enter the Chocolate Room is lifted from *The Marriage of Figaro* by **Wolfgang Amadeus Mozart** [15], and on a more contemporary note, **Marilyn Manson** [16] covered the song 'Wondrous Boat Ride' on his debut longplay *Portrait of an American Family*.

Can you also spot... Malcolm McDowell in *A Clockwork Orange*, also released in 1971 [17], Queen Elizabeth II, who is mentioned in the film [18], William Shakespeare, whose *Romeo and Juliet* is referenced [19], and *Alice in Wonderland*, which is quoted by Willy Wonka [20].

Here's a clue: middle right, in the chocolate pipe

Has The Dude given you the slip?

BEN-HUR (1959)

First published in 1880, *Ben-Hur: A Tale of the Christ* was the second novel by **Lew Wallace** [1], a decorated general from the American Civil War who led the hunt for **Billy the Kid** [2]. Wallace's book was a huge hit in its day, inspiring a popular stage play seen by over 20 million people in New York, London, Sydney and other major cities around the world. Film versions duly followed, including a 15-minute 1907 effort and a two-and-a-half hour 1925 feature starring silent era idol **Ramon Novarro** [3]. But by far the best-known adaptation arrived a little over a quarter of a century later courtesy of director **William Wyler** [4], whose ambitiously mounted project helped to re-popularize the historical adventure in Hollywood.

Despite being given a spit-polish by **Gore Vidal** [5], Karl Tunberg's original screenplay wasn't recognized at the 32nd Academy Awards in 1960. The film did manage to collect a total of 11 golden statuettes though, putting it in an elite club that counts *Titanic* and *The Lord of the Rings: The Return of the King* as its only other members. Among the individual recipients at that year's ceremony were Wyler and lead actor **Charlton Heston** [6], whose only Oscar win came from his sole nomination. **Paul Newman** [7] was offered the part of the eponymous Jewish prince, but chose to make *Exodus* instead. **Marlon Brando** [8] was also considered before Heston finally accepted, while *Naked Gun* and *Airplane!* star **Leslie Nielsen** [9] filmed a screen test for the role of Messala. And spare a thought for actor **Claude Heater** [10], who appears as Jesus Christ in the film but didn't receive a credit because he has no lines.

The chariot race scene was the brainchild of stuntman extraordinaire **Yakima Canutt** [11], a former champion rodeo rider who pioneered various action directing techniques during the golden age of the biblical epic and western genres. *Ben-Hur* was a pivotal moment in the career of another hero of the movie western, **Sergio Leone** [12], who worked as second-unit director on the film. His compatriot **Federico Fellini** [13] shot *La Dolce Vita* on the same studio backlot as *Ben-Hur*, while another renowned Italian masterwork, *The Creation of Adam* by **Michelangelo** [14] appears in the background of the film's closing credits. And speaking of the Sistine Chapel, *Ben-Hur* is the only film to earn Vatican approval in the 'religion' category. If it's good enough for **The Pope** [15] . . .

Can you also spot... Morgan Freeman in the 2016 remake [16], D-Day from *Animal House*, who says the line 'Ramming speed!' [17], William Wyler's friend and sometime collaborator Audrey Hepburn [18], the cast of *Monty Python and the Holy Grail* [19], and MGM's mascot Leo the Lion, whose famous roar was muted in the opening credits [20].

Has The Dude given you the slip? Here's a clue: lower middle, third row back above the cameraman

FERRIS BUELLER'S DAY OFF (1986)

Although he was born in Lansing, Michigan, John Hughes spent his formative years in Chicago, Illinois, shooting many of his films there. *Ferris Bueller's Day Off* is his clearest tribute to the Windy City, with many well-known landmarks, from the Art Institute where Picasso's *The Old Guitarist* [1] hangs, to Wrigley Field where the likes of **Ernie Banks** [2] wowed baseball fans with the Chicago Cubs, featured in the film. Less instantly recognizable locales include the posh restaurant that Ferris and friends blag their way into - the exact same spot where **John Belushi and Dan Aykroyd** [3] wreak havoc in their 1980 buddy comedy *The Blues Brothers*.

Hughes's film is filled with personal odes to cultural icons like **Elvis Presley** [4], whose army unit motto is emblazoned on Ferris's beret, former Roxy Music crooner **Bryan Ferry** [5] and **Morrissey** [6], who rose to fame as the frontman of The Smiths. There's a more oblique reference to a cult '80s band in the casting of Richard Edson, who played drums in Sonic Youth from 1981 to 1982, next to **Kim Gordon and Thurston Moore** [7]. Edson isn't the only one with a fascinating claim to earlier fame - Ben Stein, who plays Ferris's monotone teacher, started out as a speechwriter for President **Richard Nixon** [8]. The presidential connection doesn't end there, as former First Lady **Barbara Bush** [9] once paraphrased the film in a 1990 commencement speech at a Massachusetts college.

Few films have had such a lasting impact on popular culture as *Ferris Bueller's Day Off*. There's even a fan theory which posits that the story actually takes place inside Cameron Frye's head, which would make Ferris a **Tyler Durden-style alter ego** [10]. Alan Ruck came close to missing out on this career-making role, as Cameron was originally written with **Emilio Estevez** [11] in mind. Likewise the part of Sloane Peterson almost went to **Molly Ringwald** [12], who starred in Hughes's first two films, *Sixteen Candles* and *The Breakfast Club*. Mia Sara eventually got the gig, but not before cancelling an audition which could have seen her cast alongside **David Bowie** [13] in *Labyrinth*. But no one benefitted from the film's success more than its young lead. Despite having over 70 acting credits to his name, including voicing **Simba** [14] in Disney's *The Lion King*, **Matthew Broderick** [15] will forever be associated with the charming school-shy Chicagoan who taught us that to fully appreciate life you've got to stop and look around once in a while.

Can you also spot... Jennifer Grey in *Dirty Dancing* [16], Jeffrey Jones in *Amadeus* [17], Joe Pesci and Daniel Stern in *Home Alone* [18], Chevy Chase in *National Lampoon's Vacation* [19], 'Danke Schoen' singer Wayne Newton [20], and Florence Nightingale, who is referenced in the film [21].

Here's a clue: middle, to the right of the hotdog

Has The Dude given you the slip?

PLANET OF THE APES (1968)

Forget the so-so sequels, disastrous **Tim Burton** [1] remake and **Andy Serkis** [2] powered reboot series, as far as the *Planet of the Apes* franchise is concerned, the original is still the best. It's a film crammed with classic scenes, the most famous being the twist ending, which *The Simpsons* memorably reimagined as a Broadway musical starring resident ham **Troy McClure** [3]. Yet perhaps the most poignant moment in the film occurs when **Charlton Heston** [4] says, 'Some apes, it seems, are more equal than others' - a line ripped from another famed allegory, **George Orwell**'s [5] *Animal Farm*.

The film was written by **Rod Serling** [6], creator of TV's *The Twilight Zone*, who based his script on French author **Pierre Boulle**'s [7] 1963 science fiction novel *La Planète des Singes*, which was published in the UK as *Monkey Planet*. However, this wasn't the first Boulle story to receive the big screen treatment - his semi-autobiographical World War II drama *The Bridge Over the River Kwai* was the basis for the similarly named 1957 epic starring **William Holden** [8]. *Planet of the Apes* director Franklin J. Schaffner went on to direct a war movie of his own, *Patton*, for which **George C. Scott** [9] won the Best Actor Oscar in 1971.

Planet of the Apes was nominated for two Academy Awards, an incredibly rare honour for a sci-fi film to be bestowed with back then. As it turned out, 1968 was a good year for genre cinema, with **Stanley Kubrick**'s [10] *2001: A Space Odyssey* and George A. Romero's *Night of the Living Dead* released a few months apart. Schaffner had a lot to thank director Richard Fleischer for, as it was the success of his 1966 film *Fantastic Voyage*, about a scientist played by French character actor **Jean Del Val** [11] who discovers a way to shrink people, which convinced 20th Century Fox to green-light his primate-themed dystopian adventure.

It also helped that Schaffner had a bona fide Hollywood icon in his ranks, although everyone from **Sean Connery** [12] to **John Wayne** [13] was considered for the part of George Taylor. Heston described the filming of *Planet of the Apes* as hell in his on-set diary, but later described it as one of his favourite films. By contrast, **Ingrid Bergman** [14] claimed that turning down the part of Zira was her greatest regret. Finally, the courtroom scene was inspired by a real-life case where a Tennessee schoolteacher was arrested for teaching **Charles Darwin**'s [15] theory of evolution - further proof that we humans are often slow to catch on.

Can you also spot... King Kong [16], the Three Wise Monkeys [17], Ronald Reagan in *Bedtime for Bonzo* [18], and the young orangutan from *Dunston Checks In* [19].

Here's a clue: middle left, behind the guards on the bridge

Has The Dude given you the slip?

FOUR WEDDINGS AND A FUNERAL (1994)

Who doesn't love a good wedding movie? Remember Julia Roberts [1] hotfooting it in *The Runaway Bride*, or Dustin Hoffman's [2] bold declaration at the end of *The Graduate*. How about Toni Collette [3] walking down the aisle to ABBA in *Muriel's Wedding*, or Vince Vaughn and Owen Wilson [4] getting more than they bargained for in *The Wedding Crashers*. And who could forget Adam Sandler [5] warbling away in *The Wedding Singer*, or Steve Martin [6] losing his cool in *Father of the Bride*. Yet throughout the rich history of matrimonial cinema, arguably none has given audiences more cause for celebration than *Four Weddings and a Funeral*.

Directed by Mike Newell and written by Richard Curtis [7], the creator of such cherished TV comedies as *Blackadder* and *Mr. Bean* [8], this is in many ways the quintessential Brit flick. It boasts an impeccable cast, endlessly quotable one-liners and a chart-topping pop soundtrack that features Wet Wet Wet's cover of 'Love is All Around' by The Troggs [9], as well as Gloria Gaynor's [10] disco classic 'I Will Survive' and no fewer than three Elton John [11] jams. Remarkably, *Four Weddings and a Funeral* was the first British film since 1988's *A Fish Called Wanda*, starring John Cleese and Jamie Lee Curtis [12], to reach the No. 1 spot at the US box office. A commercial and cultural smash on both sides of the Atlantic, the film gave an added boost to the 1990s rom-com revival which - for better and for worse - would last well into the next decade.

It was also a star-making moment in the career of a young Hugh Grant [13], who prior to 1994 had mostly appeared in minor supporting roles on British television. Curtis and producer Duncan Kenworthy would cast him twice more, in 1999's *Notting Hill* and 2003's *Love Actually*, but neither film had quite the same impact as *Four Weddings and a Funeral*. At the film's glitzy Leicester Square premiere, Grant's then girlfriend Elizabeth Hurley [14] made headlines when she rocked up to the red carpet event wearing a striking black Versace dress, which she has since blamed for preventing her from becoming a more serious actress. Grant's on-screen love interest, Andie MacDowell [15], has revealed that she channelled Hollywood grande dame Katharine Hepburn [16] when developing her character. Sarah Jessica Parker [17] auditioned for the role of Carrie and was reportedly Curtis's top choice, while Marisa Tomei [18] turned down the part because she was tending to her sick grandfather in New York.

Can you also spot... Michael Douglas and Glenn Close in *Fatal Attraction*, mentioned by Andie MacDowell's character [19], Oscar Wilde, who is also namechecked [20], and Prince Charles, whose image appears in the closing credits [21].

Has The Dude given you the slip? Here's a clue: top right, in the stained glass window

THE GRAND BUDAPEST HOTEL (2014)

Martin Scorsese [1] once hailed **Wes Anderson** [2] as 'the next Scorsese' after attending a screening of his low-budget directorial debut, *Bottle Rocket*, in 1996. Yet while Anderson lists the master director of *Taxi Driver* and *Goodfellas* as a key influence on his work, his eighth feature owes much of its distinctive visual language to two earlier cinematic supremos, **Max Ophüls** [3] and **Jacques Tati** [4]. *The Grand Budapest Hotel* also contains a reference to another European art-house film in the form of Harvey Keitel's Ludwig, whose tattoos are an exact replica of those adorning the body of Père Jules in French director Jean Vigo's 1934 masterpiece *L'Atalante*.

More directly, the film ends with a dedication to the life and work of the Austrian writer **Stefan Zweig** [5], whose novella *Letter from an Unknown Woman* was adapted by Ophüls in 1948. In addition to Zweig's writings, Anderson makes several allusions to **Agatha Christie** [6] throughout his film, most notably in the naming of Saoirse Ronan's character. The Irish actress is one of several newcomers to the Anderson stable, including Tony Revolori, whose lobby boy Zero was named after the American comedy actor **Samuel Joel 'Zero' Mostel** [7], and British thespian **Ralph Fiennes** [8], who fought off competition from **Johnny Depp** [9] for the part of M. Gustave. Fiennes has revealed that he based his character's accent on that of **Leonard Rossiter** [10], the celebrated British screen and stage actor best known for TV's *Rising Damp* and his occasional collaborations with Stanley Kubrick.

Of course, *The Grand Budapest Hotel* also stars various Anderson regulars, from *Rushmore*'s **Jason Schwartzman** [11] to *The Life Aquatic with Steve Zissou*'s **Bill Murray** [12] and Jeff Goldblum, the latter having previously played a character named Kovacs in the 1984 TV movie *Between the Laughter*, a biopic of the much-loved American entertainer **Ernie Kovacs** [13]. On the surface of it you'd be forgiven for thinking that *The Grand Budapest Hotel* is the biggest American production to be both shot and set in the Hungarian capital since the classic **James Stewart/Margaret Sullivan** [14] romance, *The Shop Around the Corner*, but in fact the events of Anderson's film take place in the fictitious Republic of Zubrowka. No Wes Anderson movie would be complete without a highly stylized, chocolate-box setting, and his signature production design is enhanced in this case by the director's fondness for the likes of **Mario Prada** [15], whose fashion house provided the luggage used in the film.

Can you also spot... A boy with an apple [16], Sam and Suzy from *Moonrise Kingdom* [17], Mr. Fox from *Fantastic Mr. Fox* [18], Mordecai, the falcon from *The Royal Tenenbaums* [19], and Mia Farrow in *Rosemary's Baby*, Anderson's favourite film [20].

Here's a clue: middle left, behind the reception desk

Has The Dude given you the slip?

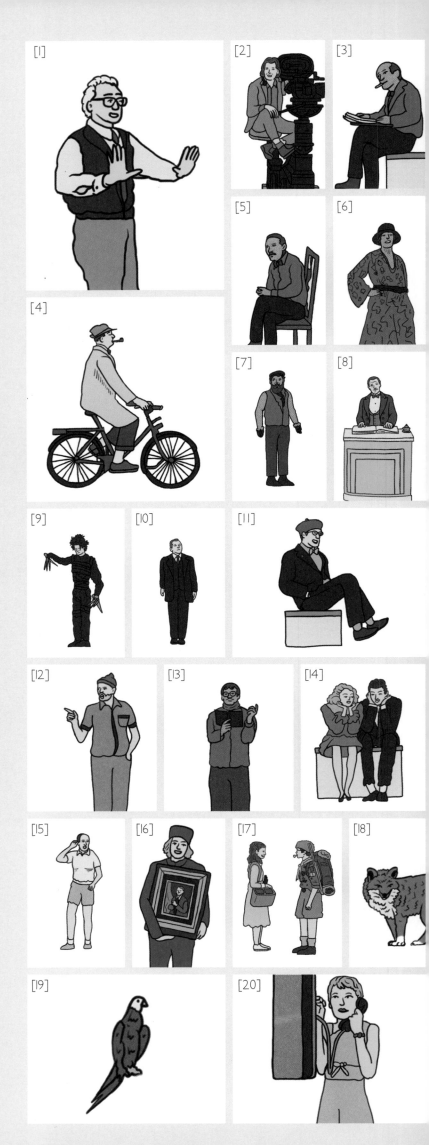

THE WIZARD OF OZ (1939)

Movie mogul **Louis B. Mayer** [1] purchased the rights to *The Wizard of Oz* from MGM co-founder Samuel Goldwyn following the success of *Snow White and the Seven Dwarfs*, which showed Hollywood that there was big money to be made from children's stories. Coincidentally, **Adriana Caselotti** [2], the young actress who voiced the title character in Disney's first ever animated feature, has a small cameo in the film.

The influence of *The Wizard of Oz* stretches as far as **Elton John** [3], who named his 1973 album *Goodbye Yellow Brick Road* after the film, and as wide as **David Lynch** [4], who drew inspiration from it for his 2001 film *Mulholland Drive*. A lesser known fact is that the rag doll costume **Dick Van Dyke** [5] wears in *Chitty Chitty Bang Bang* was modelled on the Scarecrow. While *The Wizard of Oz* has been mined by various artists over the years, it was itself based on **L. Frank Baum**'s [6] fantasy adventure novel from 1900. The film also borrowed from cinema's past, reusing a crystal ball prop from the 1932 **Boris Karloff** [7] hit *The Mask of Fu Manchu*.

The Wizard of Oz has spawned numerous sequels and spin-offs, including 1985's unofficial follow-up *Return to Oz*, directed by *Apocalypse Now* sound editor **Walter Murch** [8] and starring **Fairuza Balk** [9]. There's also *Oz: The Great and Powerful*, a strange prequel-of-sorts from 2013 with **James Franco** [10], and the even more inexplicable 1978 Motown musical *The Wiz*, which saw **Michael Jackson and Diana Ross** [11] unite as the Scarecrow and Dorothy respectively. Back to MGM's original, **Judy Garland** [12] was only cast after studio execs failed to prise child star **Shirley Temple** [13] away from 20th Century Fox. Deanna Durbin was also approached but was already contracted on another film, leaving Garland free to step into the ruby slippers. A rising star at the time, Garland became a household name virtually overnight following the film's release, aided by the overwhelming popularity of 'Over the Rainbow', the heartfelt ballad written by **Harold Arlen and Yip Harburg** [14], which Garland sang on the soundtrack.

The part of the Wizard was written with **W.C. Fields** [15] in mind, but producer Mervyn LeRoy failed to convince the veteran actor that it would be worth his while, even after offering him a $5,000 per-day salary - an astronomical fee at the time. If it was awards glory Fields was after, he was justified in his decision to swerve *The Wizard of Oz*, as the film lost out to the **Clark Gable/Vivien Leigh** [16] epic *Gone with the Wind* at the 12th Academy Awards in 1940.

Can you also spot... Liza Minnelli, Judy Garland's daughter [17], Joseph Williams, lead singer of the band Toto [18], Pink Floyd, whose record *The Dark Side of the Moon* is said to sync up with *The Wizard of Oz* [19], and Rudyard Kipling, whose poem *Mandalay* is referenced in the film [20].

Has The Dude given you the slip?
Here's a clue: middle right, beneath the Wicked Witch of the West

LAURENCE KING

Published in 2018 by
Laurence King Publishing Ltd
361-373 City Road
London EC1V 1LR

enquiries@laurenceking.com
www.laurenceking.com

This work was produced by
Laurence King Publishing Ltd, London.

A catalogue record for this book is
available from the British Library.

ISBN: 978-1-78627-264-5

Printed in China